SPANISH
First 1000 Words

Illustrated by
Rachael O'Neill

Translated by
Silvia Llaguno

CHRYSALIS CHILDREN'S BOOKS

About this book

This illustrated dictionary is just right if you are starting to learn Spanish. You will find lots of clearly labelled thematic pictures. Match up the small drawings around the main pictures to help you learn when to use each Spanish word.

Masculine and feminine words

In Spanish, some words are masculine and some are feminine. **La** in front of a word means that it is feminine and **el** comes before a masculine word:

el conejo   (masculine singular)
the rabbit

la casa   (feminine singular)
the house

When the word is plural, it has **las** or **los** in front of it:
los conejos   (masculine plural)
las casas   (feminine plural)

Accents

In Spanish, you usually stress the second to last letter of the word. When a different letter is stressed, it is marked by an accent on the vowel:

$$á \quad é \quad í \quad ó \quad ú$$

The Spanish alphabet has an additional letter – **ñ**.

ñ is pronounced as 'nya'.

This edition published in the UK in 2003 by Chrysalis Children's Books, an imprint of Chrysalis Books Group PLC, The Chrysalis Building, Bramley Road, London, W10 6SP

© Chrysalis Children's Books Group PLC

Every effort has been made to ensure none of the recommended websites in this book is linked to inappropriate material. However, due to the ever-changing nature of the Internet, the publishers regret they cannot take responsibility for future content of these websites.

British Library Cataloguing in Publication Data for this book is available from the British Library.

ISBN 1 903954 96 7 (hb)
ISBN 1 903954 97 5 (pb)

Printed and bound in China

Internet Links

1. Take an online journey through Spain:
   www.oxfam.org.uk/coolplanet/ontheline/explore/journey/spain/spindex.htm
2. Find out what Spain looks like from this lovely set of photos: **www.jtutor.clara.net/viajes/spain/spain.htm**
3. Check basic information on Spain: **www.spaintour.com/geograph.htm**
4. A nice on-line picture dictionary: **www.enchantedlearning.com/Spanish/**
5. Learn to say some useful phrases in Spanish: **www.fodors.com/language/**. Choose the sort of information you want, click on the button beside Spanish and then on a phrase to hear it spoken for you.
6. Try some translation games to see how much Spanish you've learnt: **www.syvum.com/squizzes/spanish/**
7. Learn simple phrases in Spanish and listen to how they should sound: **www.vivaspanish.org/**
8. Check out other countries that speak Spanish: **www.virtualperu.net/**
9. Try a quick quiz to see how many Spanish words you know: **www2.lhric.org/pocantico/mexico/words.htm**
10. A fascinating comparison of three cities through time – Alexandria 2000 years ago, Córdoba in Spain 1000 years ago and New York today: **www.nationalgeographic.com/3cities/**

Índice   Contents

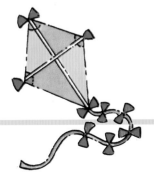

Tu ropa
Your clothes

el bolsillo
pocket

los leotardos
tights

la camiseta
T-shirt

la sudadera
sweatshirt

el cuello
collar

la camisa
shirt

el anorak
anorak

el puño
cuff

las orejeras
ear muffs

la capucha
hood

los cordones
lace

las playeras
trainers

los tirantes
braces

la camiseta interior
vest

las manoplas
mitten

los guantes
glove

la manga
sleeve

el zapato
shoe

los calzoncillos
pants

4

la bata
dressing gown

el cordón
cord

el delantal
pinafore dress

el lazo
bow

la cinta
ribbon

el ojal
buttonhole

el botón
button

la chaqueta
cardigan

la cremallera
zip

los vaqueros
jeans

la bufanda
scarf

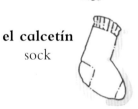

el calcetín
sock

las bragas
knickers

las sandalias
sandal

el mono
dungarees

las playeras
plimsoll

el vestido
dress

la falda
skirt

la hebilla
buckle

el cinturón
belt

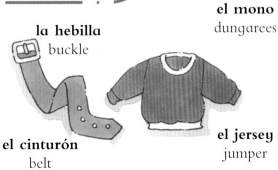

el jersey
jumper

En el dormitorio
In the bedroom

el bate de beisbol
baseball bat

la cartera
satchel

el ordenador
computer

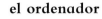

la almohada
pillow

la colcha
quilt

las zapatillas
slipper

la malla
leotard

el pijama
pyjamas

la cometa
kite

el xilófono
xylophone

el puzle
jigsaw puzzle

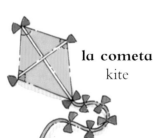

la escalera
ladder

la caja
box

el libro
book

la casa de muñecas
doll's house

el termo
Thermos flask

la mesa de escribir
desk

la percha
hanger

el tambor
drum

el espejo
mirror

el armario
wardrobe

el dibujo
drawing

las estanterias
bookcase

las sábanas
sheet

la comoda
chest of drawers

los vestidos de muñeca
doll's clothes

el tren de juguete
train set

el lápiz de color
crayon

el estuche
pencil case

el lápiz
pencil

el libro de colorear
colouring book

el castillo
castle

En el cuarto de baño
In the bathroom

la báscula
bathroom scales

la cortina de baño
shower curtain

la ducha
shower

el jabón
soap

el gorro de ducha
shower cap

la alfombrilla de baño
bath mat

la toallita
flannel

el champú
shampoo

el toallero
towel rail

la cesta de la ropa
laundry basket

la bañera
bath

el suelo de baldosas
floor tile

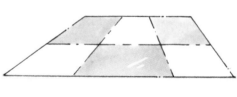

la esponja
sponge

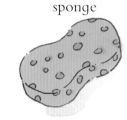

el papel higiénico
toilet paper

la taza del wáter
toilet seat

el ventilador
fan

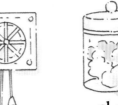

el algodón
cotton wool

el armarito de baño
cabinet

la pasta dentífrica
toothpaste

el cepillo de dientes
toothbrush

el vaso
beaker

el grifo
tap

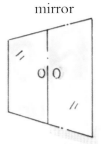

el espejo
mirror

la jabonera
soap dish

la toalla de baño
bath towel

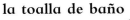
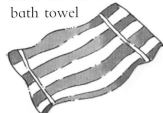

el taburete
stool

el cepillo de uñas
nailbrush

el lavabo
washbasin

el wáter
toilet

9

En la cocina
In the kitchen

el congelador
freezer

la nevera
fridge

la lavadora
washing machi

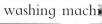

el tapón
plug

el plato
plate

la cocina
cooker

el horno
oven

la cuchara
spoon

el foco de la luz
light

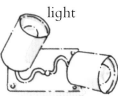

el tenedor
fork

el cuchillo
knife

la mesa
table

la ensaladera
bowl

los azulejos
tile

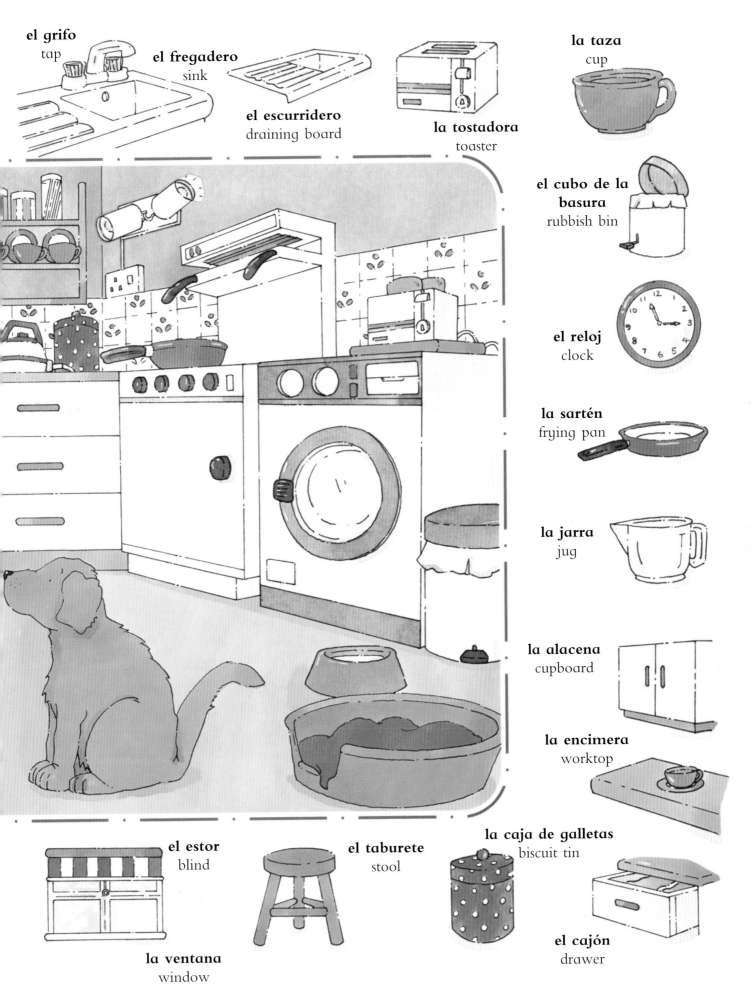

el grifo
tap

el fregadero
sink

el escurridero
draining board

la tostadora
toaster

la taza
cup

el cubo de la basura
rubbish bin

el reloj
clock

la sartén
frying pan

la jarra
jug

la alacena
cupboard

la encimera
worktop

el estor
blind

el taburete
stool

la caja de galletas
biscuit tin

el cajón
drawer

la ventana
window

11

En el salón
In the living room

el cuadro
painting

la antena
aerial

la revista
magazine

la barra de la cortina
curtain pole

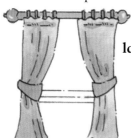

la cortina
curtain

el poyete de la ventana
windowsill

la fotografía
photograph

la vela
candlestick

la guitarra
guitar

la alfombra
rug

el tebeo
comic

el sillón
armchair

el aparato de video
video recorder

la televisión
television

el fuego
fire

el guarda fuegos
fire guard

12

la radio
radio

el radiador
radiator

el teléfono
telephone

la mesita de café
coffee table

el jarrón
vase

el altavoz
loudspeaker

el tocadiscos
record player

la grabadora
tape recorder

el lector de discos compactos
compact disc player

el mando a distancia
remote control

la pantalla de la lámpara
lampshade

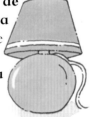
la lámpara
lamp

la repisa de la chimenea
mantlepiece

la chimenea
fireplace

la alfombra
carpet

el sofá
settee

el periódico
newspaper

la mecedora
rocking chair

13

La comida
Food

el queso
cheese

la sopa
soup

el azucar
sugar

las uvas
grape

la pera
pear

las patatas fritas
chips

la hamburguesa
hamburger

el aceite
oil

los espaguetis
spaghetti

la pimienta
pepper

la sal
salt

las espec
spice

la carne picada
mince

el huevo
egg

el café
coffee

la mermelada
jam

la miel
honey

las patatas fri
crisps

el tomate
tomato

el pepino
cucumber

el vinagre
vinegar

el ajo
garlic

la naranja
orange

el plátano
banana

la manzana
apple

el champiñon
mushroom

la patata
potato

la coliflor
cauliflower

la ciruela
plum

la cebolla
onion

**el guisante
pea**

la mantequilla
butter

os cereales
cereal

el zumo
juice

la margarina
margarine

el concentrado de zumo
squash

el arroz
rice

el pan
bread

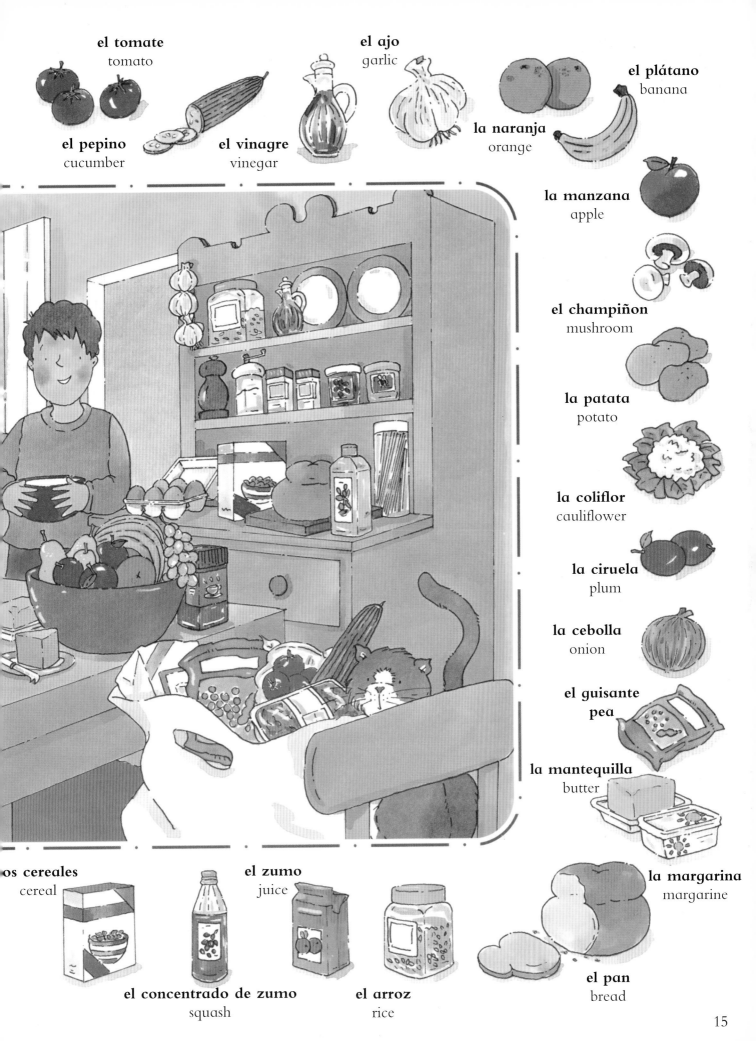

15

Las mascotas
Pets

el hueso
bone

la cama
bedding

el pico
beak

los barrotes
bar

la jaula del hamster
hamster house

el hamster
hamster

el alga
seaweed

la red metálica
wire netting

el cuenco de comida
food bowl

la cola
tail

el cachorro
puppy

la noria
wheel

la botella de agua
water bottle

el tubo
tube

la comida de perro/gato
pet/cat food

el conejo de Indias
guinea pig

el conejo
rabbit

la conejera
hutch

la jaula
cage

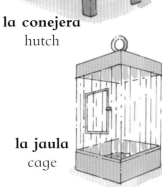

el jerbo
gerbil

la casa de pájaros
nesting box

el gatito
kitten

el pelaje
fur

la tortuga
tortoise

el ala
wing

la pata
paw

el loro
parrot

la zarpa
claw

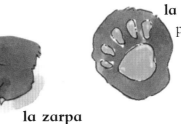

el periquito
budgerigar

Juego
Play

los patines
roller skates

el paracaidas
parachute

la venda
bandage

la nave espacial
spacecraft

el patinete
skateboard

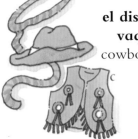

el disfraz de vaquero
cowboy outfit

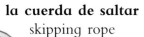

la cuerda de saltar
skipping rope

el balón de fútbol
football

el Arca de Noé
Noah's ark

el cubilete
beaker

el dado
dice

el juego de mesa
board game

las canicas
marble

el yo-yo
yo-yo

el arco
bow

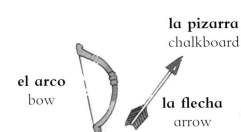

la pizarra
chalkboard

la flecha
arrow

la tiza
chalk

el Lego
Lego

la diana
target

la plasticina
Plasticine

la tienda de campaña
tent

la marioneta de trapo
glove puppet

el reloj de pulsera
watch

el castillo
castle

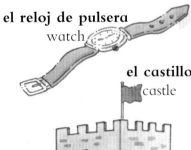

el disfraz de enfermera
nurse's outfit

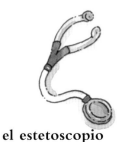

el maletín de médico
doctor's bag

el disfraz de médico
doctor's outfit

la granja de juguete
toy farm

el estetoscopio
stethoscope

19

En el jardín
In the garden

la manguera
hose

la puerta trasero
back door

el tricíclo
tricycle

el escalón
step

la gatera
cat flap

el párterre
flower bed

el borde
border

el césped
lawn

la mesa de pajaros
bird table

el cacahuete
peanut

el coco
coconut

el tocón de árbol
tree stump

diente de leon
dandelion

el muro
wall

la escoba
broom

la horca
garden for

las botas
boots

la mala hierba
weed

la familia
family

el jardín de rocas
rock garden

la fuente
waterfall

el nenúfar
waterlily

el jardín agreste
wild garden

los pájaros de jardin
garden birds

la cabaña
shed

el arbusto
shrub

el terrazo
terrace

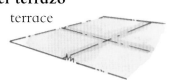

rta-césped
awnmower

el rastrillo
rake

la paleta
trowel

la pala
spade

el tiesto
flowerpot

la jardinera
window box

21

En el colegio
At school

la hoja
leaf

el mapa
map

**la lectora
el lector**
reader

el ordenador
computer

el colgador
peg

el abrigo
coat

**la mesa de
objetos naturales**
nature table

**el baúl de
los juguetes**
toy box

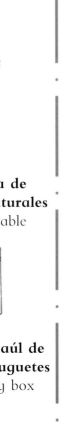

la papelera
wastepaper bin

la arcilla
clay

las pinturas
paint

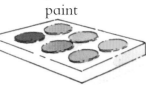

el pincel
paintbrush

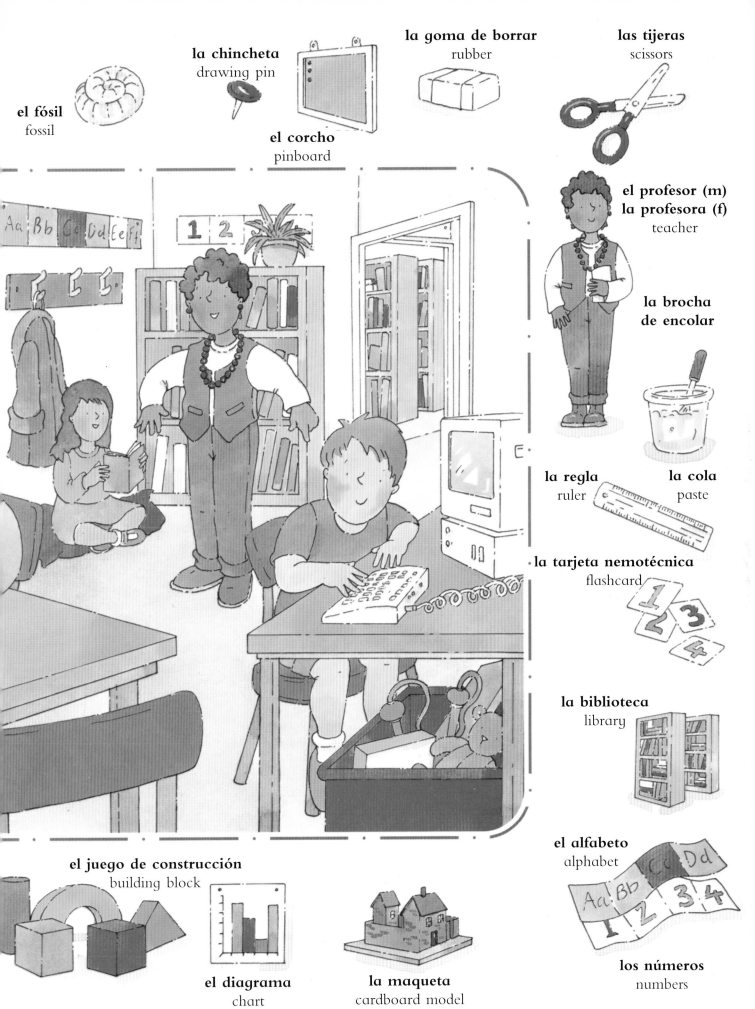

el fósil
fossil

la chincheta
drawing pin

el corcho
pinboard

la goma de borrar
rubber

las tijeras
scissors

el profesor (m)
la profesora (f)
teacher

la brocha
de encolar

la regla
ruler

la cola
paste

la tarjeta nemotécnica
flashcard

la biblioteca
library

el juego de construcción
building block

el diagrama
chart

la maqueta
cardboard model

el alfabeto
alphabet

los números
numbers

23

En el parque
In the park

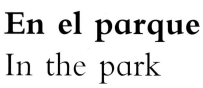

la cafeteria
café

el cochecito de bebés
pram

el terraplén
slope

la pista de tenis
tennis court

el sonajero
rattle

el bebé
baby

la sillita
pushchair

el tio-vivo
roundabout

los hierros de trepar
climbing frame

el tobogán
slide

el area de juegos
playground

el balancín
seesaw

la fosa de arena
sandpit

la correa
lead

la paloma
pigeon

la pelota de tenis
tennis ball

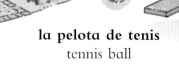

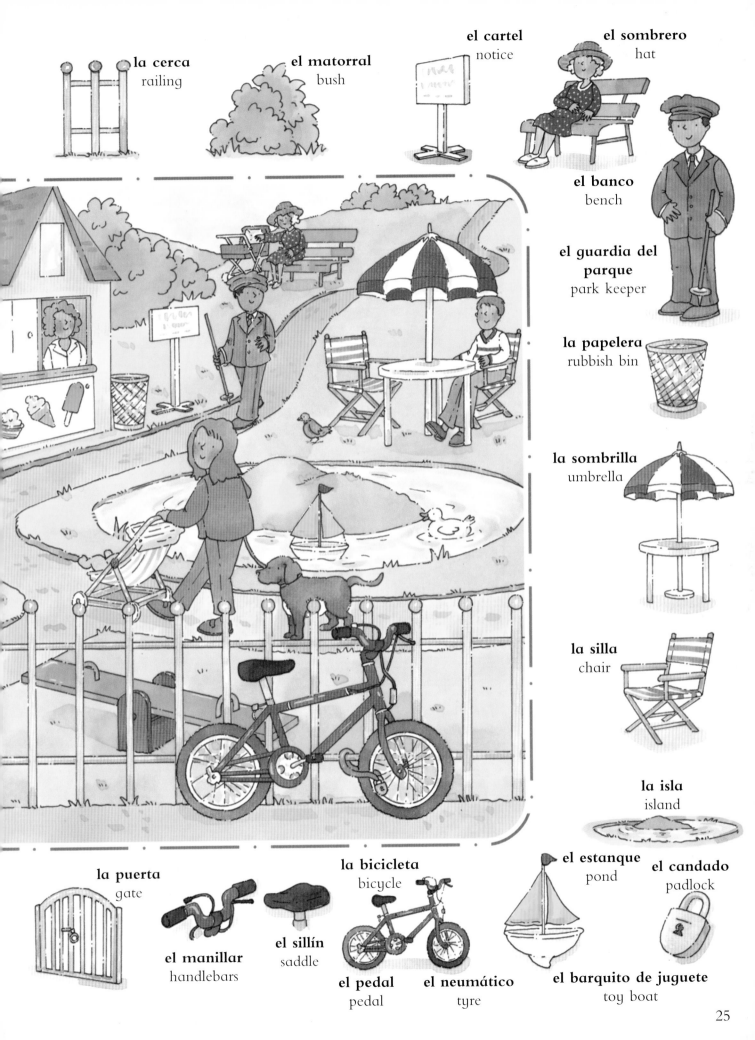

la cerca
railing

el matorral
bush

el cartel
notice

el sombrero
hat

el banco
bench

el guardia del parque
park keeper

la papelera
rubbish bin

la sombrilla
umbrella

la silla
chair

la isla
island

la puerta
gate

el manillar
handlebars

el sillín
saddle

la bicicleta
bicycle

el pedal
pedal

el neumático
tyre

el estanque
pond

el candado
padlock

el barquito de juguete
toy boat

25

En las obras
On the building site

el andamio
scaffolding

el camión-vertedero
tipper truck

el asfalto
tarmac

el bloque de pisos
tower block

la excavadora
digger

la apisonadora
steamroller

la compresora
compressor

la cargadora
loader

el albañil
bricklayer

el ladrillo
brick

el camión de descarga
dumper truck

la carretilla
wheelbarrow

la rueda
wheel

la taladradora neumática
pneumatic drill

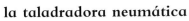
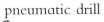

el carpintero
carpenter

la mezcladora de granito
concrete mixer

la grúa
crane

el casco de protección
safety hat

el mono de trabajo
overalls

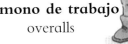

el obrero
builder

el vertedero
skip

la arena
sand

el techo
roof

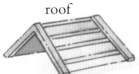

el para-brisas
windscreen

el volante
steering wheel

el tractor nivelador
bulldozer

la mezcladora de cemento
cement mixer

el coche de bomberos
fire engine

el camión semi-remolque
articulated lorry

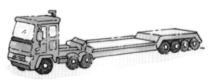

27

En la ciudad
In the town

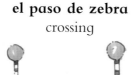

el paso de zebra
crossing

el ayuntamiento
town hall

la farola
lamp post

la ambulancia
ambulance

el hospital
hospital

el coche
car

el policia (m)
police officer

la guardia de tráfico (f)
el guardia de tráfico (m)
traffic warden

el semáforo
traffic lights

la silla de ruedas
wheelchair

la gasolinera
petrol station

el surtidor de gasolina
petrol pump

el camión
truck

28

el conductor de autobús
bus driver

el autobús
bus

la casa
house

el poste telegráfico
telegraph pole

la parada del autobus
bus stop

el garage
garage

la parada de autobús cubierta
shelter

el limpia-cristales
window cleaner

el aparcamiento
car park

el banco
bank

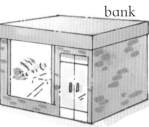

el supermercado
supermarket

la tienda
shop

la juguetería
toy shop

la cartero (f)
el cartero (m)
postman
postwoman

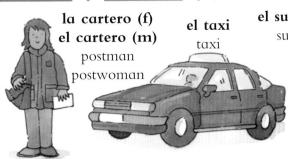

el taxi
taxi

la acera
pavement

29

En la granja
On the farm

el heno
hay

la fosa
ditch

el potro
foal

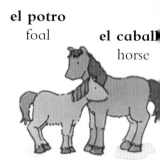

el caball
horse

el toro
bull

la pocilga
pig sty

el cerdo
pig

el cochinillo
piglet

el granero
barn

el abrevadero
trough

el perro pastor
sheepdog

el granjero
farmer

la vaca
cow

el ternero
calf

el ganso
goose

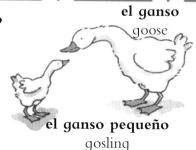

el ganso pequeño
gosling

la cuadra
stable

el espantapájaros
scarecrow

el tractor
tractor

el remolque
trailer

la gallina
hen

el pollito
chick

el gallinero
hen house

el establo
cowshed

el muro
wall

la puerta
gate

el frutal
orchard

la escalera
ladder

la oveja
sheep

el camión
truck

el patito
duckling

el pato
duck

el corral
farmyard

el cordero (m)
lamb

el lago de patos
duck pond

31

De viaje
Travelling

el globo
hot air balloon

el barco de vela
sailing boat

el lago
lake

el helicóptero
helicopter

la vela
sail

el yate
yacht

la canoa
canoe

el puente
bridge

el tunel
tunnel

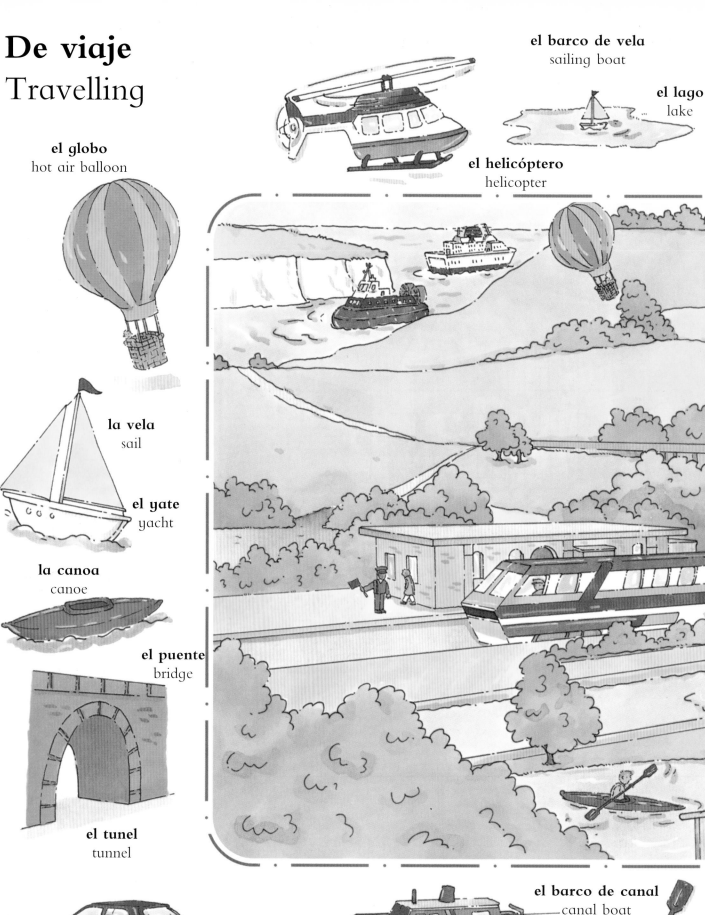

el coche
car

el barco de canal
canal boat

el canal
canal

el remo
oar

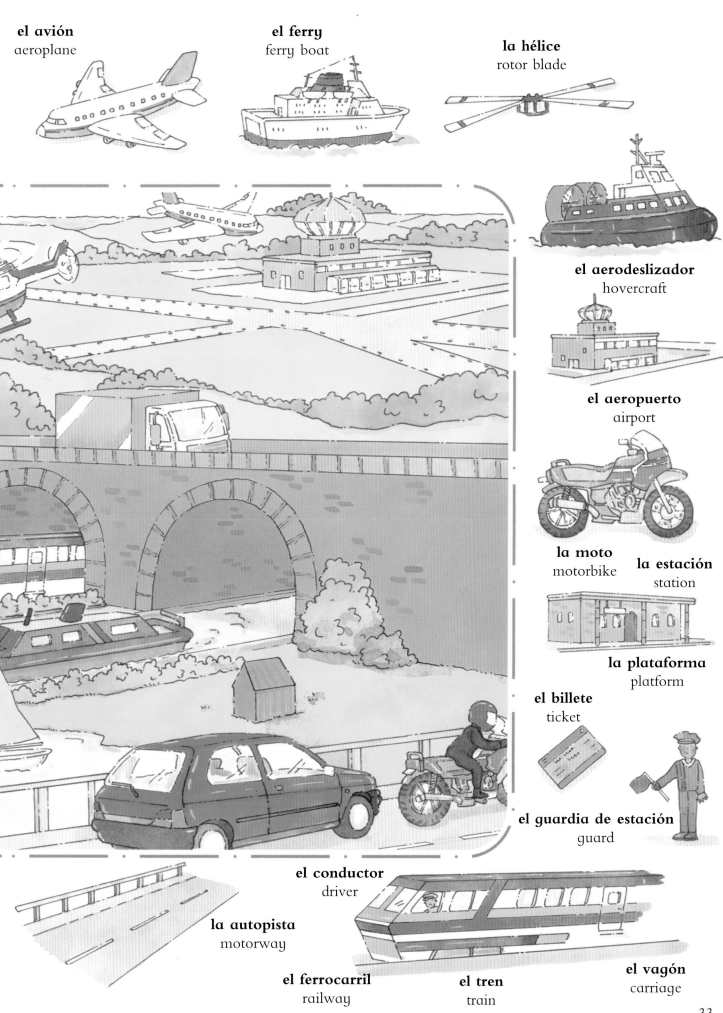

el avión
aeroplane

el ferry
ferry boat

la hélice
rotor blade

el aerodeslizador
hovercraft

el aeropuerto
airport

la moto
motorbike

la estación
station

la plataforma
platform

el billete
ticket

el guardia de estación
guard

el conductor
driver

la autopista
motorway

el ferrocarril
railway

el tren
train

el vagón
carriage

En la playa
On the beach

el mar
sea

el acantilado cliff

la butaca de playa
deckchair

la playa
beach

el parapeto
windbreak

el hotel
hotel

el bronceador
suntan lotion

las gafas de sol
sunglasses

la toalla de playa
beach towel

el cubo
bucket

la pala
spade

la pelota de playa
beach ball

la cesta de picnic
picnic basket

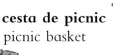
las algas
seaweed

la gamba
shrimp

el tubo respiratorio
snorkel

las gafas submarinas
goggles

los brazadores
armband

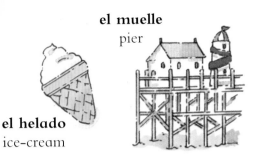

el helado
ice-cream

el muelle
pier

la red
net

los guijarros
pebble

las conchas
shell

el castillo de arena
sandcastle

el foso
moat

la bandera
flag

la ola
wave

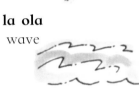

el faro
lighthouse

la tabla de windsurf
windsurfer

la tabla de surf
surfboard

las aletas
flipper

la gaviota
seagull

el chaleco salvavidas
lifejacket

la lancha motora
motor boat

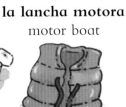

el barco de vela
sailing boat

el mástil
mast

Bajo el agua
Underwater

el buzo
diver

la foca
seal

la tortuga marina
turtle

el delfín
dolphin

la raya
ray fish

el caballito de mar
seahorse

el coral
coral

el banco de peces
shoal

la morsa
walrus

la estrella de mar
starfish

el tesoro
treasure

la gamba
shrimp

la chirla
clam

el naufragio
wreck

el cañón
cannon

botella de oxígeno
aqualung

las gafas de buzo
face mask

la linterna
torch

la ballena
whale

el traje de submarinista
wet suit

el pulpo
octopus

el tentáculo
tentacle

la ventosa
sucker

la anémona de mar
sea anemone

la cueva
cave

el pez espada
swordfish

la aleta
fin

la cigala
lobster

la medusa
jellyfish

la ostra
oyster

la anguila
eel

el tiburon
shark

37

Los animales salvajes
Wild animals

el mono
monkey

el hipopótamo
hippopotamus

la serpiente
snake

la cabra
goat

la zebra
zebra

el canguro
kangaroo

la girafa
giraffe

el pelícano
pelican

el cuerno
horn

el rinoceronte
rhinoceros

la lagartija
lizard

el camello
camel

el caimán
alligator

el león **la leona**
lion   lioness

el cachorro de león
lion cub

las astas
antlers

el ciervo
deer

el guepardo
cheetah

el tigre
tiger

la llama
llama

el avestruz
ostrich

el elefante
elephant

el leopardo
leopard

os colmillos
tusk

la trompa
trunk

el todo-terreno
van

el flamingo
flamingo

39

La fiesta
Having a party

la varita
mágica
magic wand

el mago
magician

el paq
parc

la capa
cloak

la paja
straw

el pastel
cake

las luces de
Navidad
fairy lights

el perrito caliente
hot dog

el globo
balloon

el mantel
tablecloth

la vela
candle

el plato de
cartón
paper plate

el vaso de cartón
paper cup

la servilleta de papel
paper napkin

el lazo
bow

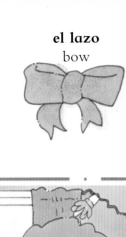

la tarjeta de felicitacioń
card

el matasuegras
party squeaker

la corona de papel
paper hat

la serpentina
streamer

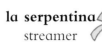

el vestido de fiesta
party dress

la sorpresa Navideña
cracker

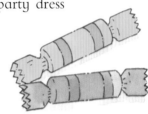

la guirlanda de papel
paper chain

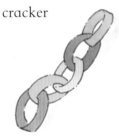

la flor de papel
paper flower

la bebida
drink

el sombrero de copa
top hat

el pañuelo
handkerchief

el regalo
present

41

El mundo de los cuentos
World of stories

el dragón
dragon

el nomo
gnome

la luna
moon

los espectadores
audience

la espada
sword

el escudo
shield

la pluma
plume

el casco
helmet

la armadura
armour

el caballero
knight

la reina
queen

el rey
king

el pirata
pirate

el mago
wizard

la olla
cauldron

el monstruo
monster

el buho
owl

42

el payaso
clown

el castillo
castle

el fantasma
ghost

el hada
fairy

el gigante
giant

el bufón
jester

el unicornio
unicorn

la corona
crown

el príncipe
prince

la princesa
princess

el palo de escoba
broomstick

la bruja
witch

la seta venenosa
toadstool

el maquillaje
make-up

el bosque encantado
enchanted wood

Las formas y los colores
Shapes and colours

gordo (m)
gorda (f)
fat

delgado (m)
delgada (f)
thin

la parte de arriba
top

la parte de abajo
bottom

arriba
up

abajo
down

estrecho
narrow

ancho
wide

contento (m)
contenta (f)
happy

triste
sad

duro (m)
dura (f)
hard

blando (m)
blanda (f)
soft

nuevo (m)
nueva (f)
new

viejo (m)
vieja (f)
old

naranja
orange

verde
green

púpura
purple

gris
grey

rosa
pink

blanco (m)
blanca (f)
white

azul
blue

amarillo
yellow

negro (m)
negra (f)
black

marrón
brown

rojo (m)
roja (f)
red

el rectángulo
rectangle

el cuadrado
square

la estrella
star

el círculo
circle

la esfera
sphere

el cubo
cube

el triángulo
triangle

corto (m)
corta (f)
short

grande
tall

pequeño (m)
pequeña (f)
short

largo (m)
larga (f)
long

el arco-iris
rainbow

Las estaciones
Seasons

el árbol de hoja perenne
evergreen tree

el trineo
sledge

el muñeco de nieve
snowman

el copo de nieve
snowflake

la nieve
snow

la rama
branch

la bola de nieve
snowball

el nido
nest

las flores
blossom

el cordero
lamb

la tormenta
rain shower

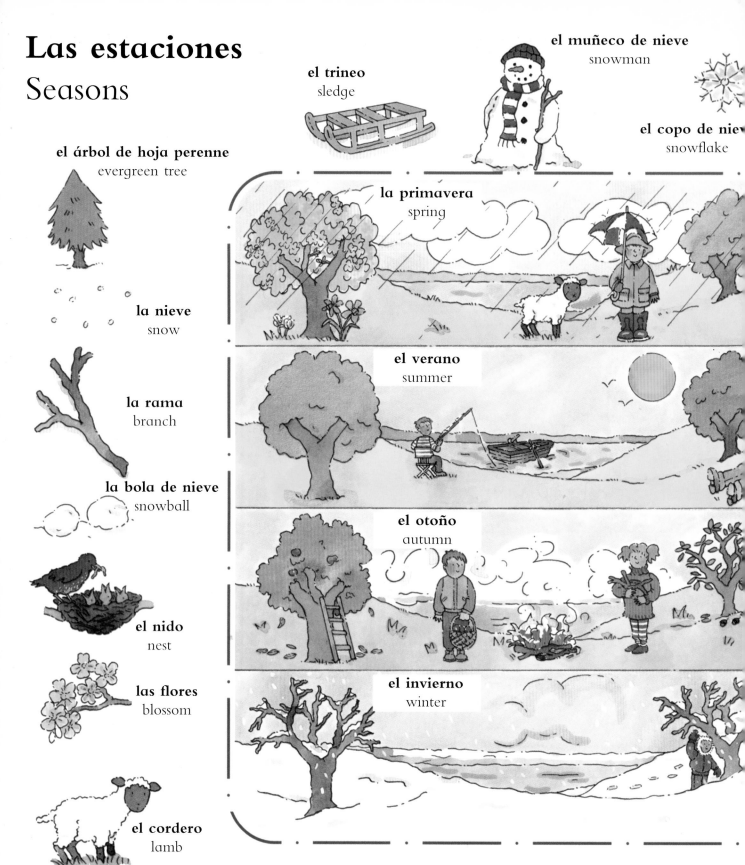

la primavera
spring

el verano
summer

el otoño
autumn

el invierno
winter

el capullo
bud

la flor del azafrán
crocus

el narciso
daffodil

la primavera
primrose

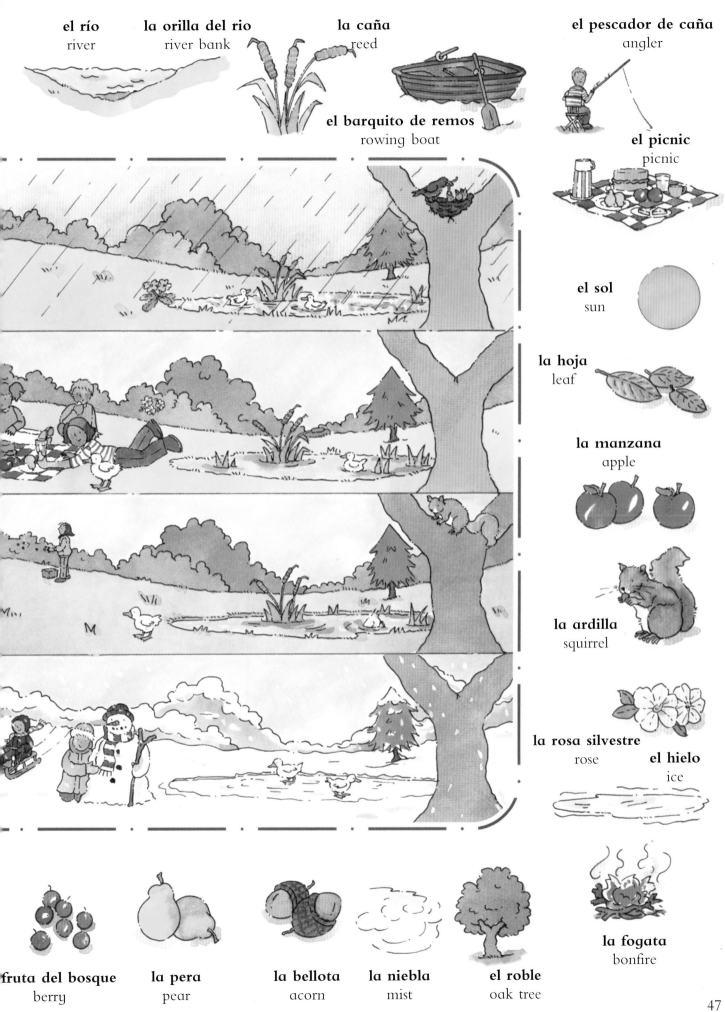

el río
river

la orilla del rio
river bank

la caña
reed

el pescador de caña
angler

el barquito de remos
rowing boat

el picnic
picnic

el sol
sun

la hoja
leaf

la manzana
apple

la ardilla
squirrel

la rosa silvestre
rose

el hielo
ice

la fogata
bonfire

fruta del bosque
berry

la pera
pear

la bellota
acorn

la niebla
mist

el roble
oak tree

Los días de la semana
Days of the week

lunes	martes	miércoles	jueves	viernes
Monday	Tuesday	Wednesday	Thursday	Friday

sábado	**domingo**	**el fin de semana**
Saturday	Sunday	the weekend

Los meses del año
Months of the year

enero	abril	julio	octubre
January	April	July	October
febrero	**mayo**	**agosto**	**noviembre**
February	May	August	November
marzo	**junio**	**septiembre**	**diciembre**
March	June	September	December

1	2	3	4	5	6	7	8	9	10
uno	dos	tres	cuatro	cinco	seis	siete	ocho	nueve	diez

11	12	13	14	15	16	17	18	19	20
once	doce	trece	catorce	quince	dieciseis	diecisiete	dieciocho	diecinueve	veinte

21	22	23	24	25
ventiuno	ventidos	ventitres	venticuatro	venticinco

30	40	50	60	70	80	90
treinta	cuarenta	cincuenta	sesenta	setenta	ochenta	noventa

100	1,000	1,000,000
cien	mil	un millón